Hugo's Simplified System

German Verbs
Simplified

Hugo's Language Books Ltd

This enlarged edition
© 1987 Hugo's Language Books Ltd
All rights reserved
ISBN 0 85285 122 7

3rd Impression 1991

This edition revised by

Naomi Laredo BA (Cantab)

Set in 9/11pt Linotron 202 Times by
Typesetters Limited, Stanstead Abbotts, Herts
Printed and bound in Great Britain by
Courier International Ltd, Tiptree, Essex

Preface

This book sets out in an easy-to-use form all the information you need to be able to use the German regular and irregular verbs correctly in all tenses and persons. The greater part of the book is intended for reference only and thus includes far more detail than Hugo's 'German in Three Months', which teaches only what is essential for a basic grasp of the language. However, to simplify the learning process for beginners, the most important points for practical purposes are emphasised throughout. Where certain details are of less importance in everyday conversation and could be left until a later stage, this is indicated.

Contents

Structure of a verb

A verb expresses an action or a state of being. The verb is the most important part of speech in any language, and should therefore be learned as thoroughly as possible. If you are a little uncertain about its general structure, the following notes may help to refresh your memory.

In this book you will find tables showing the conjugations of German verbs. To conjugate a verb means to show all its different forms.

Verbs can be *transitive* or *intransitive*. Transitive verbs are so called because they transmit the action from the subject to the object. Intransitive verbs convey a complete meaning without the addition of an object. *Roger hit* conveys no special meaning, but *Roger* (subject) *hit* (verb) *the car* (object) is a complete sentence. The verb *hit* is transitive. *It rains, she smiles*, make sense without the addition of an object. The verbs *rains, smiles* are intransitive.

Many verbs can be transitive or intransitive depending on their use in a particular sentence. *I'm singing* is intransitive, but *I'm singing a song* is transitive. *He grew* is intransitive, *he grew a beard*, transitive.

Verbs consist of two *voices* (active and passive), four *moods* (infinitive, indicative, subjunctive and imperative), three principal *tenses* (present, past, future), two *numbers* (singular and plural), and three *persons* in each number (1st, 2nd and 3rd).

In the *active* voice, the subject of the verb is the doer of the action expressed: *Susan* (subject) *is eating* (verb). The active voice often expresses a state or condition: *the river flows, the children rest.* In the passive voice, the subject receives the action expressed: *The apple was eaten, the car was hit.*

Of the four moods, the *infinitive* is the word given in the dictionary (in English it is recognised by the word *to: to go, to stay*) and is in effect the name of the verb. It expresses the action itself, without any reference to time or to the person doing the action.

7

The *indicative* is by far the most used mood. It indicates or expresses a thing as a fact in present, past, or future time, rather than as a wish or a possibility; these are indicated by the *subjunctive,* which has almost completely disappeared in English and is rarely used in German.

The *imperative* mood is used for giving an order or command. The imperative has only one tense, the present, and only two persons, the 2nd (*you*) person singular and plural.

If a verb has only one person or thing as its subject, its *number* is *singular.* If it has more than one person or thing as its subject, its number is *plural.* *I'm studying* is singular; *They're fighting* is plural. The 1st person is identified by the personal pronouns *I* and *we*; the 2nd person by *you* (singular and plural), and the 3rd person by *he*, *she, it,* and *they.* Tenses are always arranged in the following order:

1st person singular	I paint
2nd person singular	you paint
3rd person singular	he, she, it paints
1st person plural	we paint
2nd person plural	you paint
3rd person plural	they paint

The German verb

German verbs are really very simple, as there are only two true tenses to be learnt: the present and the past. The other tenses are compound, as in English: that is, they are formed from a combination of more than one word, for example:

Ich habe gesehen (perfect tense)
I have seen

Ich werde gehen (future tense)
I shall go

The past participle, which is used in the formation of the perfect and conditional tenses, is the other major part of the verb which must be learnt.

Within each tense, the only really important persons to learn are the 1st and 3rd persons singular and plural – and in the present tense the plural forms are identical to the infinitive and to the imperative (polite form). (The sole exception to this is the verb *sein*, 'to be'.) The 2nd person of the verb is the familiar form of address, which is of little practical use to the student; the polite form of address is identical to the 3rd person plural and so is easy to learn.

The subjunctive is rarely used except in indirect (also called reported) speech, and its formation can be learnt after the indicative has been mastered.

In the reference tables of complete model conjugations in this book we give all the parts of the verb necessary to form any person, tense and mood. As the formation of the compound tenses, the passive mood and the reflexive, negative and interrogative forms is precisely the same for any verb in the language, these are not given in full.

The list of irregular verbs at the end of the book gives the major parts of almost every irregular verb in the current language, but for practical purposes only the most common – which are marked with an asterisk – need be learnt at first.

Subject pronouns

Before studying the verbs it is useful to look at the subject pronouns, which are always closely linked with them. This will help to clarify the use of each person of the verb. The subject pronouns in German are:

	Singular		Plural	
1st pers.	*ich*	I	*wir*	we
2nd pers.	*du*	you (familiar sing.)	*ihr*	you (familiar pl.)
	Sie	you (polite sing.)	*Sie*	you (polite pl.)
3rd pers.	*er*	he	*sie*	they
	sie	she		
	es	it		

The familiar pronouns *du* (in the singular) and *ihr* (in the plural) are only used when talking to members of your immediate family, close friends, children and animals. (*Du* also corresponds to the biblical and poetic 'thou' and *ihr* to 'ye'.) Most students will therefore be using *Sie,* the polite form for both singular and plural, most of the time.

Although *Sie* means 'you' and is properly speaking a 2nd person form, it is followed by the 3rd person plural form of the verb (the same as for *sie,* 'they'). In the sections on regular and auxiliary verbs which follow, we shall therefore concentrate on the first and third persons singular and plural, since these are the most used.

Regular verbs

This section gives only the most important persons and tenses. Other parts of the verbs are dealt with separately, and complete model conjugations are given later in the book for reference.

Infinitive

The infinitive of almost all German verbs ends in *en*. The few exceptions are *sein* (to be), *tun* (to do) and a few verbs ending in either *eln* or *ern*. For regular verbs, removing the ending *en* or *n* gives the stem. This is invariable and is used to form the different tenses and persons of the verb by adding the various endings. For example:

Infinitive:	*fragen*	to ask	Stem:	*frag-*
	machen	to do, make		*mach-*
	lächeln	to smile		*lächel-*
	wandern	to go walking		*wander-*

The subsections below show the endings to be added to form the present and past tenses, taking *fragen* as our model.

Present indicative tense

ich frage	I ask	*wir* ⎫		we ⎫	
er fragt	he asks	*Sie* ⎬ *fragen*		you ⎬ ask	
		sie ⎭		they ⎭	

(Familiar 2nd person forms: *du fragst; ihr fragt* or *ihr fraget*.)

As you can see, the plural in both 1st and 3rd persons is identical to the infinitive.

Verbs ending in *eln* omit the *e* before the *l* in the first person singular, and verbs ending in *ern* may optionally omit the *e*. For example:

ich lächle	I smile	*ich wandere* or *wandre*	I go walking
er lächelt	he smiles	*er wandert*	he goes walking
sie lächeln	they smile	*sie wandern*	they go walking

Note that the German present tense is the equivalent of both the English simple present tense (I ask) and present progressive tense (I am asking). This is explained more fully in the section on the 'Present participle'.

Past indicative tense

$\left.\begin{array}{l}ich \\ er\end{array}\right\}$ *fragte* $\left.\begin{array}{l}I \\ he\end{array}\right\}$ asked $\left.\begin{array}{l}wir \\ Sie \\ sie\end{array}\right\}$ *fragten* $\left.\begin{array}{l}we \\ you \\ they\end{array}\right\}$ asked

(Familiar 2nd person forms: *du fragtest; ihr fragtet.*)

This tense is the equivalent of the English simple past (I asked) and past progressive (I was asking). See the section on the 'Present participle' below.

Insertion of 'e'

After certain stems it is sometimes difficult to pronounce the present and past tense endings, and when this happens an *e* is inserted before the ending. This generally occurs in the 3rd person singular of the present tense (and also the familiar 2nd person forms) and in all persons of the past tense, when the stem ends in *d* or *t*, or in *m* or *n* preceded by a different consonant. For example:

Infinitive		Stem	Forms with *e*
baden	to bathe	*bad-*	*er badet*
			ich badete, wir badeten etc.
verachten	to despise	*veracht-*	*er verachtet*
			ich verachtete, wir verachteten etc.
öffnen	to open	*öffn-*	*er öffnet*
			ich öffnete, wir öffneten etc.

Infinitive	Stem	Forms with *e*
atmen to breathe	*atm-*	*er atmet*
		ich atmete, wir atmeten etc.

Actually the insertion of 'e' also often occurs in English, for the same reasons. For example, we say: I ask, he asks; I come, he comes; but: I miss, he misses; I push, he pushes.

Auxiliary verbs

The three verbs *sein* (to be), *haben* (to have) and *werden* (to become) are known as auxiliary verbs because they help to form the compound tenses of all the German verbs. (They are also used as verbs in their own right, of course.) It is therefore important to learn them thoroughly. All three are irregular verbs.

Sein

PRESENT TENSE:

ich bin	I am	*wir* ⎫		we ⎫	
er ist	he is	*Sie* ⎬	*sind*	you ⎬	are
		sie ⎭		they ⎭	

(Familiar 2nd person forms: *du bist; ihr seid.*)

Note that *sein* is the only German verb in which the plural of the present tense is not the same as the infinitive.

PAST TENSE:

ich ⎫	*war*	I ⎫	was	*wir* ⎫		we ⎫	
er ⎭		he ⎭		*Sie* ⎬	*waren*	you ⎬	were
				sie ⎭		they ⎭	

(Familiar 2nd person forms: *du warst; ihr wart* or *waret.*)

Haben

PRESENT TENSE:

ich habe	I have	*wir* ⎫		we ⎫	
er hat	he has	*Sie* ⎬	*haben*	you ⎬	have
		sie ⎭		they ⎭	

(Familiar 2nd person forms: *du hast; ihr habt* or *habet.*)

$$\left.\begin{array}{l} ich \\ er \end{array}\right\} hatte \quad \left.\begin{array}{l} I \\ he \end{array}\right\} had \qquad \left.\begin{array}{l} wir \\ Sie \\ sie \end{array}\right\} hatten \quad \left.\begin{array}{l} we \\ you \\ they \end{array}\right\} had$$

(Familiar 2nd person forms: *du hattest; ihr hattet.*)

Werden

PRESENT TENSE:

$$\begin{array}{ll} ich\ werde & I\ become \\ er\ wird & he\ becomes \end{array} \qquad \left.\begin{array}{l} wir \\ Sie \\ sie \end{array}\right\} werden \quad \left.\begin{array}{l} we \\ you \\ they \end{array}\right\} become$$

(Familiar 2nd person forms: *du wirst; ihr werdet.*)

PAST TENSE:

$$\left.\begin{array}{l} ich \\ er \end{array}\right\} wurde \quad \left.\begin{array}{l} I \\ he \end{array}\right\} became \qquad \left.\begin{array}{l} wir \\ Sie \\ sie \end{array}\right\} wurden \quad \left.\begin{array}{l} we \\ you \\ they \end{array}\right\} became$$

(Familiar 2nd person forms: *du wurdest; ihr wurdet.*)

Participles

Past participle

In English the past participle of regular verbs ends in 'ed', as in 'I have asked', 'he has opened' etc. In German regular verbs form their past participles by adding *ge* to the beginning of the stem and *t* to the end of it. For example:

Infinitive		Stem	Past participle	
fragen	to ask	*frag-*	*gefragt*	asked
hören	to hear	*hör-*	*gehört*	heard
lächeln	to smile	*lächel-*	*gelächelt*	smiled

Again, whenever the *t* ending is difficult to pronounce (see under 'Regular verbs' above) an *e* is inserted before it. For example:

Infinitive		Stem	Past participle
baden	to bathe	*bad-*	*gebadet*
öffnen	to open	*öffn-*	*geöffnet*
atmen	to breathe	*atm-*	*geatmet*

There are two groups of verbs which are exceptions to this general pattern and do not add the prefix *ge*. The first is the group of verbs which already begin with a unaccented prefix (*be-, emp-, er-, ge-, miß-, ver-, zer-* etc.). For example:

Infinitive		Stem	Past participle
erzählen	to tell (story)	*erzähl-*	*erzählt*
behandeln	to treat	*behandel-*	*behandelt*
verachten	to despise	*veracht-*	*verachtet*

The second is the group of verbs which end in *ieren*. These are words of foreign origin and are stressed on the *ie* of the ending. For example:

Infinitive		Stem	Past participle
regieren	to govern	*regier-*	*regiert*
studieren	to study	*studier-*	*studiert*

For irregular past participles see the list of irregular verbs at the end of this book. Most irregular past participles end in *en*.

The past participle is used in German, as in English, to form the perfect tenses (perfect, pluperfect and future perfect) and the conditional tenses (conditional and conditional perfect). The formation of these tenses is described in the section on 'Compound tenses' below.

Present participle

The present participle is the form of the verb which in English ends in 'ing': 'asking', 'opening' etc. In German it is formed by adding *d* to the infinitive:

fragen	to ask	*fragend*	asking
lächeln	to smile	*lächelnd*	smiling
verachten	to despise	*verachtend*	despising
studieren	to study	*studierend*	studying

The only exception to this rule is:

sein	to be	*seiend*	being

Note that the present participle is not used in exactly the same way in German and English. In German it is never used after the verb 'to be' to make a progressive form, as in English. The English progressive tenses (I am walking, he was laughing etc.) are translated in German by the simple present, past etc. tenses. For example:

they are bathing	becomes	they bathe	*sie baden*
he is breathing		he breathes	*er atmet*
she was laughing		she laughed	*sie lachte*
I was studying		I studied	*ich studierte*

The German present participle may be used as an adjective, as a noun or in a participial clause. Here are examples of each of these uses:

> *ein weinendes Kind*
> a weeping child

ein Reisender/eine Reisende
a traveller (= a travelling person)

lachend ging er hinaus
he went out laughing

Compound tenses

The formation of the compound tenses is very similar in English and German. Again, only the major persons of each tense are given here; for the full forms see the complete model conjugations later in this book.

Future

The future tense is formed by placing the present tense of *werden* before the infinitive. (*Werden* is thus the equivalent of English 'shall' or 'will' here.)

ich werde fragen	I shall ask	*wir werden fragen*	we shall ask
er wird fragen	he will ask	*sie werden fragen*	they will ask

This is the same for all German verbs, whether regular or irregular.

In English we often talk about the future by using the present progressive tense (I am going to Germany next year, I am seeing my mother tomorrow etc.). Similarly, in German the simple present tense can be used to refer to the future. For example:

ich fahre morgen nach Berlin
I am travelling to Berlin tomorrow

er kommt um neun Uhr an
he is arriving at nine o'clock

Conditional

The conditional is formed by placing before the infinitive *würde* for the singular and *würden* for the plural. (*Würde* and *würden* are actually past subjunctive forms of *werden*; here they are the equivalent of English 'should' or 'would'.)

ich würde fragen	I should ask	*wir würden fragen*	we should ask
er würde fragen	he would ask	*sie würden fragen*	they would ask

Again, this applies to every German verb.

Perfect and pluperfect

These tenses are usually formed exactly as in English, using the verb *haben* (to have) followed by the past participle. The present tense of *haben* is used for the perfect, the past tense for the pluperfect.

PERFECT:

ich habe gefragt	I have asked	*wir haben gefragt*	we have asked
er hat gefragt	he has asked	*sie haben gefragt*	they have asked

PLUPERFECT:

ich hatte gefragt	I had asked	*wir hatten gefragt*	we had asked
er hatte gefragt	he had asked	*sie hatten gefragt*	they had asked

The perfect and pluperfect of *sein, werden* and certain other verbs are formed with *sein* instead of *haben*. These are mostly verbs which express movement (e.g. *gehen*, to go; *fliegen*, to fly) or a change of state (e.g. *aufwachen*, to wake up; *sterben*, to die) – plus the verb *bleiben*, to remain. In the list of irregular verbs at the end of this book, those which take *sein* are indicated. Examples:

ich bin gewesen	I have been	*wir sind geworden*	we have become
er war gekommen	he had come	*sie waren gegangen*	they had gone

These verbs only take *sein* when they are used intransitively – that is, without a direct object. When there is a direct object they take *haben*. For example:

ich bin mit der Eisenbahn gefahren
I travelled by train

ich habe das Auto gefahren
I drove the car

ich habe selbst gefahren
I myself drove (the object *Auto* is understood here)

As you can see from the above examples and their translations, the perfect tense is often used in German where in English we would use the simple past tense. It is used when the effects of a past action or event are still felt in the present, so it is generally used in preference to the simple past tense when talking about the immediate past.

Future perfect and conditional perfect

These tenses are again formed in the same way as the English equivalents, but there is a difference in word order between the two languages. The future perfect is formed with the present tense of *werden* plus the past participle <u>followed by</u> the infinitive of *haben* (or *sein*); in English the infinitive comes first:

ich werde gefragt haben	I shall have asked
er wird gegangen sein	he will have gone
wir werden studiert haben	we shall have studied

The conditional perfect is formed with *würde* (singular) or *würden* (plural) plus the past participle again followed by the infinitive of *haben* (or *sein*).

ich würde gefragt haben	I should have asked
er würde gegangen sein	he would have gone
wir würden studiert haben	we should have studied

The rule for which verbs take *sein* instead of *haben* is the same for these tenses as for the perfect and pluperfect tenses (see above).

Word order

When the compound tenses are used in a sentence the word order differs from English. The auxiliary is separated from the rest of the verb construction, which goes to the end of the sentence or clause. In the future tense and the conditional it is the infinitive which goes to the end:

Ich werde das Haus verkaufen, wenn . . .
I shall sell the house when . . .

Ich würde das Haus verkaufen, wenn . . .
I should sell the house if . . .

In the perfect and pluperfect tenses it is the past participle:

Er ist nach Berlin gefahren.
He (has) travelled to Berlin.

Er hatte die Frage nicht beantwortet, als . . .
He had not answered the question, when . . .

In the future perfect and conditional perfect both the past participle and
the infinitive go to the end – and as we have seen, the infinitive follows
the past participle, the reverse of the English order:

Er wird mit ihr gegangen sein.
He will have gone with her.

Ich würde auf der Universität studiert haben, wenn . . .
I should have studied at the university if . . .

Modal verbs

Use and formation

Modal verbs are used in conjunction with another verb to express obligation, ability, willingness etc. They are rarely used on their own. These are the German modal verbs, with their English equivalents:

dürfen   to be allowed to (I may)
können   to be able to (I can)
mögen   to like to
müssen   to be obliged to (I must)
sollen   to ought to (I should)
wollen   to be willing to, want to

Note that to express prohibition (must not) *dürfen* is used rather than *müssen*. This can be confusing for English students. Compare the following examples:

wir müssen	*wir dürfen*
we must, we are obliged to	we may, we are allowed to
wir müssen nicht	*wir dürfen nicht*
we need not, we are not obliged to	we may not, we are not allowed to

For more about the negative form, see the section 'Negative form' below.

Note also that *mögen* is not the only way of expressing liking. When talking about activities they like, Germans more often use the word *gern* (gladly) rather than the modal verb *mögen*. And when talking about things and particularly people they like, the verb *gefallen* (to please) is generally used. Examples:

ich schwimme gern or less commonly *ich mag schwimmen*
I like swimming

er gefällt mir or less commonly *ich mag ihn*
I like him

The modal verbs are all irregular in the singular of the present tense and several of them are also slightly irregular in the past. The forms are given below.

PRESENT:

ich er	darf	wir sie	dürfen
ich er	kann	wir sie	können
ich er	mag	wir sie	mögen
ich er	muß	wir sie	müssen
ich er	soll	wir sie	sollen
ich er	will	wir sie	wollen

The letter *ß* in *muß* is simply another way of writing *ss*. It is generally used at the end of a word or syllable, and in certain other circumstances, but it is possible to write *ss* instead.

The familiar 2nd person forms are *du darfst, ihr dürft; du kannst, ihr könnt;* etc.

PAST:

All the modal verbs which have an umlaut (*ä, ö, ü*) in the infinitive lose this in the past tense.

ich er	durfte	wir sie	durften
ich er	konnte	wir sie	konnten
ich er	mochte	wir sie	mochten

ich $\Big\}$ er	mußte	wir $\Big\}$ sie	mußten
ich $\Big\}$ er	sollte	wir $\Big\}$ sie	sollten
ich $\Big\}$ er	wollte	wir $\Big\}$ sie	wollten

PAST PARTICIPLE:

The umlaut is again lost in the past participle:

dürfen	gedurft
können	gekonnt
mögen	gemocht
müssen	gemußt
sollen	gesollt
wollen	gewollt

In practice these past participles are rarely used, as they are almost always replaced by the infinitive; see the following subsection on 'Infinitive for past participle'.

FUTURE:

ich werde können etc.   I shall be able to etc.

CONDITIONAL:

ich würde können etc.   I should be able to etc.

PERFECT:

ich habe können (or *gekonnt*) etc. I have been able to etc.

PLUPERFECT:

ich hatte können (or *gekonnt*) etc. I had been able to etc.

FUTURE PERFECT:

ich werde gekonnt haben (or   I shall be able to etc.
    haben können etc).

ich würde gekonnt haben (or   I should have been able to etc.
   haben können) etc.

Infinitive for past participle

When the modal verbs are used with another infinitive – as is almost always the case – the past participle of the modal is replaced by its infinitive. For example:

ich habe es tun können (not *gekonnt*)
I have been able to do it

er hatte nicht kommen dürfen (not *gedurft*)
he had not been allowed to come

The same happens to other verbs when they are used, like modal verbs, with another infinitive. Common examples are:

brauchen   to need (to do)
heißen   to order (s.o. to do)
helfen   to help (s.o. to do)
hören   to hear (s.o. doing)
lassen   to have (sth. done)
lehren   to teach (s.o. to do)
lernen   to learn (to do)
sehen   to see (s.o. doing)

wir haben ihn nicht springen sehen (not *gesehen*)
we did not see him jump

ich habe mir neue Stiefel machen lassen (not *gelassen*)
I have had some new boots made for me

Main verb omitted

Quite often the main verb is actually omitted from a sentence with a modal verb, as the meaning is felt to be clear without it. Examples:

ich muß weg (= *ich muß weggehen*)
I must go away

er konnte es (= *er konnte es tun*)
he was able to (do it)

When the main infinitive is omitted and the modal verb is in a compound tense, the past participle of the modal is often used, rather than being replaced with the infinitive as described in the subsection above. But even in these cases the infinitive of the modal verb is sometimes substituted:

er hat es gekonnt (or *er hat es können*)
he has been able to do it

wir haben nicht anders gedurft (or *wir haben nicht anders dürfen*)
we have not been allowed to do otherwise

As a foreigner, you are advised to play safe and make your meaning clearer by not omitting the main verb in these cases.

Question form

Asking a question in German is very simple. In English we have to add the auxiliary verb 'do' to most verbs to form a question: for example, 'I ask' becomes 'do I ask?'. The exceptions are auxiliary verbs such as 'have' and 'be': 'have I?', 'am I?'. In German all verbs can form questions by this simple inversion of subject and verb. Here are the question forms in the present tense:

frage ich?	do I ask?	*fragen wir?*	do we ask?
fragst du?	do you ask?	*fragt ihr?*	do you ask?
	(familiar)		(familiar)
fragt er?	does he ask?	*fragen Sie?*	do you ask? (polite)
		fragen sie?	do they ask?

In the compound tenses the subject and the auxiliary verb are inverted; the infinitive or past participle, as always, goes to the end of the clause or sentence. For example:

werde ich ... fragen?	shall I ask ...?
habe ich ... gefragt?	have I asked ...? *or* did I ask ...?

The same pattern occurs when there is a modal verb:

darf ich ... fragen?	may I ask ...?
wollen sie ... fragen?	do they want to ask ...?

When the question is introduced by a question word (what, who, when etc.) this is placed at the beginning of the sentence and then the same pattern follows. Here are some examples:

Wann kommen Sie nach Deutschland?
When are you coming to Germany?

Warum haben Sie mich gestern angerufen?
Why did you ring me up yesterday?

Wer will heute abend ins Kino gehen?
Who wants to go to the cinema this evening?

Negative form

Making a negative statement or question is also simpler in German than in English. English uses the auxiliary 'do' to form negatives with all verbs except auxiliary verbs: for example, 'I don't like', 'he doesn't smoke'. German simply adds the word *nicht* or another negative word to the sentence:

ich frage nicht	I do not ask	*wir fragen nicht*	we do not ask
du fragst nicht (familiar)	you do not ask	*ihr fragt nicht* (familiar)	you do not ask
er fragt nicht	he does not ask	*Sie fragen nicht* (polite)	you do not ask
		sie fragen nicht	they do not ask

As a general rule *nicht* (or another negative word) follows the verb – or the auxiliary or modal verb if there is one – and any direct object. Here are some examples:

Ich sehe sie nicht oft.
I don't see her often.

Ich habe dieses Buch nie gelesen.
I have never read this book.

Ich will nicht wissen, was er gesagt hat.
I don't want to know what he said.

In questions the subject and verb are inverted as usual (see the previous section) and *nicht* etc. follows in its usual place:

Sieht er sie nicht oft?
Doesn't he see her often?

Haben Sie dieses Buch noch nicht gelesen?
Haven't you read this book yet?

Will sie nicht wissen, was er gesagt hat?
Doesn't she want to know what he said?

Imperative mood

The polite form of the imperative, which is all that need concern most students, is simply formed by adding *Sie* after the infinitive. This is the same for both singular and plural. Examples:

fragen Sie!
ask!

gehen Sie!
go!

For the familiar forms of the imperative, singular and plural, see the section below on 'Second person familiar forms'.

The following are not strictly imperative forms, although they are usually classified as such. The 1st person plural can be rendered in various ways:

gehen wir
wir wollen gehen   let us go
lassen Sie uns gehen

In the 3rd person *sollen* is used for the imperative:

er soll gehen
let him go, he is to go

sie sollen es tun
let them do it, they are to do it

(If 'let' means simply 'allow' or 'permit' and is not an imperative, *lassen* is used: *lassen sie ihn gehen,* let him go, allow him to go.)

Subjunctive mood

The subjunctive mood has been left until this point in the book for two reasons: it is not very commonly used, and its formation follows a regular pattern and so is quite easy to learn.

Formation

PRESENT TENSE:

This is formed, for both regular and irregular verbs, by adding to the stem *e* for the 1st and 3rd persons singular and *en* for the 1st and 3rd persons plural. (For the 2nd person see the section on 'Second person familiar forms' below.) Examples:

fragen	to ask	ich er	*frage*	wir sie	*fragen*
lächeln	to smile	ich er	*läch(e)le*	wir sie	*läch(e)len*
haben	to have	ich er	*habe*	wir sie	*haben*
werden	to become	ich er	*werde*	wir sie	*werden*
können	to be able to	ich er	*könne*	wir sie	*können*

The sole exception is:

sein	to be	ich er	*sei*	wir sie	*seien*

PAST TENSE:

In all regular verbs this is exactly the same as the past indicative. For example:

31

fragen to ask	$\left.\begin{array}{l} ich \\ er \end{array}\right\}$ *fragte*	$\left.\begin{array}{l} wir \\ sie \end{array}\right\}$ *fragten*

The past subjunctive of irregular verbs only differs from the past indicative (which can be found in the table of irregular verbs at the end of this book) in two points:

1. *a*, *o* or *u* add an umlaut and become *ä*, *ö* or *ü*;
2. an *e* is added to the singular form, unless the indicative already ends in *e*.

Here are some examples:

	Past indicative		Past subjunctive	
	Singular	Plural	Singular	Plural
spoke	*sprach*	*sprachen*	*spräche*	*sprächen*
found	*fand*	*fanden*	*fände*	*fänden*
carried	*trug*	*trugen*	*trüge*	*trügen*
was	*war*	*waren*	*wäre*	*wären*
wrote	*schrieb*	*schrieben*	*schriebe*	*schrieben*
had	*hatte*	*hatten*	*hätte*	*hätten*
could	*konnte*	*konnten*	*könnte*	*könnten*
liked	*mochte*	*mochten*	*möchte*	*möchten*

Exceptions are the past subjunctive forms of *sollen* and *wollen*, which do not add an umlaut. They are therefore the same as the past indicative:

should	*sollte*	*sollten*	*sollte*	*sollten*
wanted	*wollte*	*wollten*	*wollte*	*wollten*

A few other irregular verbs have past subjunctive forms in which the vowel is different from the past indicative. These are shown in the list of irregular verbs at the end of the book.

COMPOUND TENSES:

The subjunctive of the compound tenses is formed in the same way as the indicative, except that the <u>subjunctive</u> of the relevant auxiliary (*werden, haben* or *sein*) in the relevant tense is used. So, for example:

er werde fragen   (future subjunctive)
er habe gefragt, er sei gegangen   (perfect subjunctive)
er hätte gefragt, er wäre gegangen   (pluperfect subjunctive)
er werde gefragt haben   (future perfect subjunctive)

Use

The subjunctive mood is used in certain specific constructions. The major ones are the following:

First, in indirect (also called reported) speech: that is, when statements or questions are reported, but the exact words are not quoted. In this case the verb of the dependent sentence (the reported speech) is made subjunctive. For example:

er sagte, er sei zu alt or *er sagte, daß er zu alt sei*
he said he was too old

ich fragte, wer es wisse
I asked who knew it

sie fragte, warum er nicht komme
she asked why he did not come

(If the exact words are quoted, the subjunctive is of course not used: *seine Worte waren, 'Ich bin zu alt'; ich sagte, 'Wer weiß das?'* etc.)

Notice that the tenses are different in English and German in the above examples. In German the tendency is to report something said in the present tense in the present subjunctive, so the present is usual in sentences like this. But it would also be correct to use the past subjunctive, giving:

er sagte, er wäre zu alt or *er sagte, daß er zu alt wäre*
ich fragte, wer es wüßte
sie fragte, warum er nicht käme

Second, the past subjunctive is often used instead of the conditional, especially when the modal verbs are involved, because it is neater. Thus, for example:

Was täten Sie in einem solchen Falle?   (subjunctive)
or *Was würden Sie in einem solchen Falle tun?*   (conditional)
What would you do in such a case?

Wir könnten nicht kommen.   (subjunctive)
or *Wir würden nicht kommen können.*   (conditional)
We should not be able to come.

Similarly, the pluperfect subjunctive often replaces the conditional perfect:

Was hätten Sie in einem solchen Falle getan?   (subjunctive)
or *Was würden Sie in einem solchen Falle getan haben?*
  (conditional)
What would you have done in such a case?

Wir hätten nicht kommen können.   (subjunctive)
or *Wir würden nicht haben kommen können.*   (conditional)
We should not have been able to come.

Third, the past subjunctive is generally used in conditions, where the conjunction 'if' (whether expressed or understood) is followed in English by the past tense. (These are known as unreal conditions: that is, what is expressed in the condition has not actually taken place.) The subjunctive is used in the condition and the conditional in the main clause, for example:

wenn sie dort wäre, (so) würde ich sie fragen
if she were there, I should ask her

wenn Sie alles wüßten, (so) würden Sie es nicht tun
if you knew all, you would not do it

hätte ich ihn vorher gesehen, (so) wäre das nicht geschehen
had I seen him before, that would not have happened
(= if I had seen him before, ...)

As an alternative, it is possible to use the conditional in both clauses in this type of sentence, giving, for example:

wenn sie dort sein würde, so würde ich sie fragen
wenn Sie alles wissen würden, (so) würden Sie es nicht tun

In the same general category comes the use of the subjunctive in wishes, such as:

Käme er doch bald!
If only he would come soon!

Gott sei Dank!
Thanks be to God!

As a fourth category, the subjunctive is often used after verbs expressing uncertainty, whether it be probability or doubt. Some common verbs of this type are:

annehmen (daß)   to assume (that)
behaupten (daß)   to maintain (that)
fürchten (daß)   to fear (that)
glauben (daß)   to believe (that)
hoffen (daß)   to hope (that)
zweifeln (daß or *ob)* to doubt (that *or* whether)

ich glaubte, daß er dort wäre or *sei*
I believed he was there

ich hoffte, daß er bald käme or *komme*
I hoped he would come soon

Note however that the indicative can follow these verbs, when the meaning is not uncertainty, but certainty or near certainty. It follows that the subjunctive is more common in the past than the present, and more common after the 2nd and 3rd than after the 1st person. Some examples with the indicative are:

ich glaube, daß er dort ist
I believe he is there

ich hoffe, daß er bald kommt
I hope (and expect) that he will come soon

Finally, the subjunctive is often used in tentative statements and is thus used in polite requests. The past subjunctive of *können* (to be able to) equates to the English 'could' and the past subjunctive of *mögen* (to like) to the English 'should like' or 'would like'. Examples:

Könnten Sie mir bitte den Koffer tragen?
Could you please carry my case (for me)?

Ich möchte eine Tasse Tee.
I should like a cup of tea.

Passive voice

In the passive voice, as explained in the introductory section 'Structure of a verb', the subject of the verb is not the doer of the action, but the receiver of the action expressed by the verb. For example:

The apple was eaten.
The house has been sold.
The car will be repaired tomorrow.

Formation with werden

The German passive is formed in a very similar way to the English. In English we use 'to be' plus the past participle of the main verb. German uses the verb *werden* (to become) plus the past participle. A complete model conjugation is given in the tables later in the book, but here are some examples to enable you to compare the English and German constructions:

ich werde gefragt
I am being asked

das Haus wurde gekauft
the house was bought

die Studenten sind geprüft worden
the students have been examined

In the last example there are two points to note: *werden* forms its perfect tense with *sein*, as mentioned under 'Auxiliary verbs' above; and when *werden* is being used as a passive auxiliary its past participle is *worden*, not *geworden*.

When a sentence in the perfect passive refers to what is still a present state, *worden* is often omitted:

| *das Haus ist verkauft worden* | becomes | *das Haus ist verkauft* |
| the house has been sold | | the house is (now) sold |

In fact, *worden* is always omitted in this tense with the verb *gebären* (to bear), past participle *geboren*:

> *ich bin am 1. September geboren*
> I was born on 1st September

Statal passive with sein

What is known as the 'statal' passive describes a state of affairs rather than an event. In English the two are often indistinguishable:

> the house was (being) built in the valley (= statement of action in progress)
> the house was built in the valley (= description of house in existence)

In German the former is the true passive (or actional passive) which we have already seen, formed with *werden*; the latter, the statal passive, is formed with *sein*:

> *das Haus wurde im Tal gebaut*
> the house was (being) built in the valley

> *das Haus war im Tal gebaut*
> the house was built in the valley

The statal passive emphasises the completion of an action or process. It follows that it is always used in the imperative, which is, however, rare:

> *sei gegrüßt, du liebes Kind!*
> greetings (*literally* be greeted), dear child!

Second person familiar forms

As explained under the heading 'Subject pronouns', the familiar *du* and *ihr* forms are only used when speaking to immediate family, close friends, children and animals. Using them in the wrong circumstances can give offence, so you are advised to use the polite *Sie* form if in doubt.

The familiar forms for each tense are given below.

Present tense

SINGULAR:

The 2nd person singular is formed in the indicative by changing the *t* of the 3rd person singular to *st*:

er fragt	he asks	*du fragst*	you ask
er lächelt	he smiles	*du lächelst*	you smile
er öffnet	he opens	*du öffnest*	you open

This also applies to most irregular verbs: that is, where there is a vowel change in the 3rd person singular, it also happens in the 2nd person:

geben   to give   *ich gebe, du gibst, er gibt*

In the modal verbs and the irregular verb *wissen* (to know), where the 3rd person does not end in *t*, the 2nd person is simply formed by adding *st*, or just *t* if the 3rd person ends in *ß*:

er soll	he should	*du sollst*	you should
er muß	he must	*du mußt*	you must
er weiß	he knows	*du weißt*	you know

Note the forms of the auxiliary verbs:

sein	to be	*ich bin, du bist, er ist*
haben	to have	*ich habe, du hast, er hat*
werden	to become	*ich werde, du wirst, er wird*

Occasionally an *e* is inserted before the *st* ending, giving for example *du fragest.* In the present subjunctive this *e* is obligatory:

> *du fragest*
> *du läch(e)lest*
> *du öffnest*

The 2nd person plural is formed in the indicative by changing the *en* or *n* of the 3rd person plural to *t*. Sometimes the *e* is retained to make the ending easier to pronounce, as we saw with the 3rd person forms under 'Regular verbs'. Examples:

sie fragen	they ask	*ihr fragt*	you ask
sie lächeln	they smile	*ihr lächelt*	you smile
sie öffnen	they open	*ihr öffnet*	you open

This also applies to irregular verbs, modal verbs and most of the auxiliaries, but note the irregular form for sein:

sein	to be	*wir sind, ihr seid, sie sind*

As in the singular, an *e* is occasionally inserted before the ending (giving for example *ihr fraget*) and must be retained in the subjunctive:

ihr fraget
ihr läch(e)let
ihr öffnet

The irregular form for *sein* is *ihr seid*.

Past tense

SINGULAR:

The 2nd person singular is formed in the indicative by adding *st* to the 3rd person singular form:

er fragte	he asked	*du fragtest*	you asked
er lächelte	he smiled	*du lächeltest*	you smiled
er öffnete	he opened	*du öffnetest*	you opened

Again this applies to irregular verbs, and any vowel change is retained in the 2nd person, e.g. *geben: er gab, du gabst.* It also applies to the auxiliary and modal verbs, for example:

er war	he was	*du warst*	you were
er konnte	he was able to	*du konntest*	you were able to

The subjunctive is formed in the same way, but by adding the *st* ending to the 3rd person singular subjunctive form. In the regular verbs this is identical to the indicative, but in the irregular verbs it generally differs (see the section on the 'Subjunctive mood' above). For example:

	Past indicative	Past subjunctive
spoke	*er sprach, du sprachst*	*er spräche, du sprächest*
was, were	*er war, du warst*	*er wäre, du wärest*
had	*er hatte, du hattest*	*er hätte, du hättest*

Remember that *sollen* and *wollen* are exceptions and do not add an umlaut.

PLURAL:

The plural is formed in the indicative by changing the *n* of the 3rd person plural to *t*:

sie fragten	they asked	*ihr fragtet*	you asked
sie lächelten	they smiled	*ihr lächeltet*	you smiled
sie öffneten	they opened	*ihr öffnetet*	you opened

The *e* of the ending is often omitted in the irregular verbs, where this does not make pronunciation difficult. For example:

sie gaben	they gave	*ihr gabt*	you gave
sie waren	they were	*ihr wart* (or *waret*)	you were

Like the singular, the plural of the subjunctive is formed in the same way but taking the 3rd person plural of the subjunctive as its starting point. Again the regular verb forms are identical to the indicative but the irregular verb forms differ (apart from *sollen* and *wollen*):

	Past indicative	Past subjunctive
spoke	*sie sprachen, ihr spracht*	*sie sprächen, ihr sprächet*

	Past indicative	Past subjunctive
were	*sie waren, ihr wart*	*sie wären, ihr wäret*
had	*sie hatten, ihr hattet*	*sie hätten, ihr hättet*

Imperative

Unlike the polite imperative (see the section 'Imperative mood' above) the familiar imperative, singular and plural, is used without the pronouns *du* or *ihr*. The formation is given below.

SINGULAR:

In regular verbs and most irregular verbs the singular imperative consists of the stem with the ending *e*. However, this *e* is often omitted, especially in speech. Examples:

Infinitive		Stem	Imperative	
fragen	to ask	*frag-*	*frage!* or *frag!*	ask!
lächeln	to smile	*lächel-*	*lächle!*	smile!
öffnen	to open	*öffn-*	*öffne!*	open!
laufen	to run (irreg.)	*lauf-*	*laufe!* or *lauf!*	run!

The imperative of *sein* (to be) is *sei!* (be!).

Irregular verbs whose vowel changes to *i* or *ie* in the 2nd person singular (see list of irregular verbs) form the imperative from this 2nd person form, without the *st* ending:

geben	to give	*du gibst*	*gib!*	give!
lesen	to read	*du liest*	*lies!*	read!

Werden is an exception to this rule, forming its imperative like the regular verbs:

werden	to become	*du wirst*	*werde!*	become!

The imperative singular of *sehen* often ends in *e*: *siehe!* or *sieh!* see!

The plural imperative is much simpler, being exactly the same as the indicative *ihr* form (but without the pronoun):

fragen	to ask	*ihr fragt*	*fragt!* ask!
lächeln	to smile	*ihr lächelt*	*lächelt!* smile!
öffnen	to open	*ihr öffnet*	*öffnet!* open!
laufen	to run	*ihr lauft*	*lauft!* run!
geben	to give	*ihr gebt*	*gebt!* give!
lesen	to read	*ihr lest*	*lest!* read!
werden	to become	*ihr werdet*	*werdet!* become!
sein	to be	*ihr seid*	*seid!* be!

Complete model conjugations

In these tables we give you, for reference, all the forms you need to be able to conjugate a German auxiliary or regular verb fully. We do not give all the persons throughout the compound tenses, since they always follow the same pattern, as explained under 'Compound tenses' above.

Sein

INFINITIVE:

sein   *to be*

PRESENT PARTICIPLE:

seiend   *being*

PAST PARTICIPLE:

gewesen   *been*

PRESENT INDICATIVE TENSE:

ich bin	*I am*	wir sind	*we are*
du bist	*you are (fam. sing.)*	ihr seid	*you are (fam. pl.)*
er ist	*he is*	Sie sind	*you are (polite sing./pl.)*
		sie sind	*they are*

PAST INDICATIVE TENSE:

ich war	*I was*	wir waren	*we were*
du warst	*you were (fam. sing.)*	ihr war(e)t	*you were (fam. pl.)*
er war	*he was*	Sie waren	*you were (polite sing./pl.)*
		sie waren	*they were*

FUTURE INDICATIVE TENSE:

ich werde ⎫
du wirst ⎬ sein   *I shall be etc.*
er wird ⎭

wir werden ⎫
ihr werdet ⎬ sein   *we shall be etc.*
Sie werden ⎪
sie werden ⎭

CONDITIONAL TENSE:

ich würde			wir würden		
du würdest	} sein	*I should be*	ihr würdet	} sein	*we should be*
er würde		*etc.*	Sie würden		*etc.*
			sie würden		

PERFECT INDICATIVE TENSE:

ich bin *etc.* gewesen   *I have been etc.*

PLUPERFECT INDICATIVE TENSE:
ich war *etc.* gewesen   *I had been etc.*

FUTURE PERFECT INDICATIVE TENSE:

ich werde, du wirst *etc.* gewesen sein   *I shall have been etc.*

CONDITIONAL PERFECT TENSE:

ich würde *etc.* gewesen sein   *I should have been etc.*

IMPERATIVE MOOD:

sei!   *be! (fam. sing.)*
seid!   *be! (fam. pl.)*
seien Sie!   *be! (polite sing./pl.)*

PRESENT SUBJUNCTIVE TENSE:

ich sei	wir seien
du seiest	ihr seid
er sei	Sie seien
	sie seien

PAST SUBJUNCTIVE TENSE:

ich wäre	wir wären
du wärest	ihr wäret
er wäre	Sie wären
	sie wären

FUTURE SUBJUNCTIVE TENSE:

ich werde		wir werden	
du werdest	sein	ihr werdet	sein
er werde		Sie werden	
		sie werden	

PERFECT SUBJUNCTIVE TENSE:

ich sei *etc.* gewesen

PLUPERFECT SUBJUNCTIVE TENSE:

ich wäre *etc.* gewesen

FUTURE PERFECT SUBJUNCTIVE TENSE:

ich werde, du werdest *etc.* gewesen sein

Haben

INFINITIVE:

haben   *to have*

PRESENT PARTICIPLE:

habend   *having*

PAST PARTICIPLE:

gehabt   *had*

PRESENT INDICATIVE TENSE:

ich habe	*I have*	wir haben	*we have*
du hast	*you have (fam. sing.)*	ihr hab(e)t	*you have (fam. pl.)*
er hat	*he has*	Sie haben	*you have (polite sing./pl.)*
		sie haben	*they have*

PAST INDICATIVE TENSE:

ich hatte	*I had*	wir hatten	*we had*
du hattest	*you had*	ihr hattet	*you had (fam. pl.)*
	(fam. sing.)	Sie hatten	*you had (polite sing./pl.)*
er hatte	*he had*	sie hatten	*they had*

FUTURE INDICATIVE TENSE:

ich werde		wir werden	
du wirst } haben	*I shall*	ihr werdet } haben	*we shall have*
er wird	*have etc.*	Sie werden	*etc.*
		sie werden	

CONDITIONAL TENSE:

ich würde		wir würden	
du würdest } haben	*I should*	ihr würdet } haben	*we should have*
er würde	*have*	Sie würden	*etc.*
	etc.	sie würden	

PERFECT INDICATIVE TENSE:

ich habe, du hast *etc.* gehabt   *I have had etc.*

PLUPERFECT INDICATIVE TENSE:

ich hatte *etc.* gehabt   *I had had etc.*

FUTURE PERFECT INDICATIVE TENSE:

ich werde, du wirst *etc.* gehabt haben   *I shall have had etc.*

CONDITIONAL PERFECT TENSE:

ich würde *etc.* gehabt haben   *I should have had etc.*

IMPERATIVE MOOD:

hab(e)!   *have! (fam. sing.)*
hab(e)t!   *have! (fam. pl.)*
haben Sie!   *have! (polite sing./pl.)*

PRESENT SUBJUNCTIVE TENSE:

ich habe	wir haben
du habest	ihr habet
er habe	Sie haben
	sie haben

PAST SUBJUNCTIVE TENSE:

ich hätte	wir hätten
du hättest	ihr hättet
er hätte	Sie hätten
	sie hätten

FUTURE SUBJUNCTIVE TENSE:

ich werde ⎫	wir werden ⎫
du werdest ⎬ haben	ihr werdet ⎬ haben
er werde ⎭	Sie werden ⎪
	sie werden ⎭

PERFECT SUBJUNCTIVE TENSE:

ich habe, du habest *etc.* gehabt

PLUPERFECT SUBJUNCTIVE TENSE:

ich hätte *etc.* gehabt

FUTURE PERFECT SUBJUNCTIVE TENSE:

ich werde, du werdest *etc.* gehabt haben

Werden

INFINITIVE:

werden   *to become*

PRESENT PARTICIPLE:

werdend   *becoming*

PAST PARTICIPLE:

geworden   *become*
  (worden *when used as a passive auxiliary, see below*)

PRESENT INDICATIVE TENSE:

ich werde *I become*	wir werden *we become*	
du wirst *you become*	ihr werdet *you become (fam. pl.)*	
(fam. sing.)	Sie werden *you become*	
er wird *he becomes*	*(polite sing./pl.)*	
	sie werden *they become*	

PAST INDICATIVE TENSE:

ich wurde *I became*	wir wurden *we became*
du wurdest *you became*	ihr wurdet *you became (fam. pl.)*
(fam. sing.)	Sie wurden *you became (polite*
er wurde *he became*	*sing./pl.)*
	sie wurden *they became*

FUTURE INDICATIVE TENSE:

ich werde, du wirst *etc.* werden   *I shall become etc.*

CONDITIONAL TENSE:

ich würde *etc.* werden   *I should become etc.*

PERFECT INDICATIVE TENSE:

ich bin *etc.* geworden   *I have become etc.*

PLUPERFECT INDICATIVE TENSE:

ich war *etc.* geworden   *I had become etc.*

FUTURE PERFECT INDICATIVE TENSE:

ich werde, du wirst *etc.* geworden sein   *I shall have become etc.*

CONDITIONAL PERFECT TENSE:

ich würde *etc.* geworden sein   *I should have become etc.*

IMPERATIVE MOOD:

werde!   *become! (fam. sing.)*
werdet!   *become! (fam. pl.)*
werden Sie!   *become! (polite sing./pl.)*

PRESENT SUBJUNCTIVE TENSE:

ich werde	wir werden
du werdest	ihr werdet
er werde	Sie werden
	sie werden

PAST SUBJUNCTIVE TENSE:

ich würde	wir würden
du würdest	ihr würdet
er würde	Sie würden
	sie würden

FUTURE SUBJUNCTIVE TENSE:

ich werde, du werdest *etc.* werden

PERFECT SUBJUNCTIVE TENSE:

ich sei *etc.* geworden

PLUPERFECT SUBJUNCTIVE TENSE:

ich wäre *etc.* geworden

FUTURE PERFECT SUBJUNCTIVE TENSE:

ich werde, du werdest *etc.* geworden sein

Regular verb: fragen

INFINITIVE:

fragen   *to ask*

PRESENT PARTICIPLE:

fragend   *asking*

PAST PARTICIPLE:

gefragt   *asked*

PRESENT INDICATIVE TENSE:

ich frage	*I ask*	wir fragen	*we ask*
du fragst	*you ask*	ihr frag(e)t	*you ask (fam. pl.)*
	(fam. sing.)	Sie fragen	*you ask (polite sing./pl.)*
er fragt	*he asks*	sie fragen	*they ask*

PAST INDICATIVE TENSE:

ich fragte	*I asked*	wir fragten	*we asked*
du fragtest	*you asked*	ihr fragtet	*you asked (fam. pl.)*
	(fam. sing.)	Sie fragten	*you asked (polite sing./pl.)*
er fragte	*he asked*		
		sie fragten	*they asked*

FUTURE INDICATIVE TENSE:

ich werde, du wirst *etc.* fragen   *I shall ask etc.*

CONDITIONAL TENSE:

ich würde *etc.* fragen   *I should ask etc.*

PERFECT INDICATIVE TENSE:

ich habe, du hast *etc.* gefragt   *I have asked etc.*

Remember that some verbs form their perfect, pluperfect, future perfect and conditional perfect tenses with *sein* instead of *haben*.

PLUPERFECT INDICATIVE TENSE:

ich hatte *etc.* gefragt   *I had asked etc.*

FUTURE PERFECT INDICATIVE TENSE:

ich werde, du wirst *etc.* gefragt haben   *I shall have asked etc.*

CONDITIONAL PERFECT TENSE:

ich würde *etc.* gefragt haben   *I should have asked etc.*

IMPERATIVE MOOD:

frag(e)!   *ask! (fam. sing.)*
frag(e)t!   *ask! (fam. pl.)*
fragen Sie!   *ask! (polite sing./pl.)*

PRESENT SUBJUNCTIVE TENSE:

ich frage	wir fragen
du fragest	ihr fraget
er frage	Sie fragen
	sie fragen

PAST SUBJUNCTIVE TENSE:

ich fragte	wir fragten
du fragtest	ihr fragtet
er fragte	Sie fragten
	sie fragten

FUTURE SUBJUNCTIVE TENSE:

ich werde, du werdest *etc.* fragen

PERFECT SUBJUNCTIVE TENSE:

ich habe, du habest *etc.* gefragt

PLUPERFECT SUBJUNCTIVE TENSE:

ich hätte *etc.* gefragt

FUTURE PERFECT SUBJUNCTIVE TENSE:

ich werde, du werdest *etc.* gefragt haben

Reflexive verb: sich wärmen

Reflexive verbs are those which describe an action carried out by the subject upon itself. Often verbs which are reflexive in German are also reflexive in English, for example:

sich wärmen   to warm oneself
sich waschen   to wash oneself *or* get washed
sich ankleiden   to dress oneself *or* get dressed

Sometimes, however, they are not:

sich erinnern   to remember
sich bedenken   to consider
sich befinden   to be situated

We shall take *sich wärmen* as our model.

INFINITIVE:

sich wärmen   *to warm oneself*

PRESENT INDICATIVE TENSE:

ich wärme mich	*I warm myself*	wir wärmen uns	*we warm ourselves*
du wärmst dich	*you warm yourself (fam. sing.)*	ihr wärmt euch	*you warm yourselves (fam. pl.)*
er wärmt sich	*he warms himself*	Sie wärmen sich	*you warm yourself* or *yourselves (polite sing./pl.)*
sie wärmt sich	*she warms herself*	sie wärmen sich	*they warm themselves*

PAST INDICATIVE TENSE:

ich wärmte mich *etc.*   *I warmed myself etc.*

FUTURE INDICATIVE TENSE:

ich werde mich, du wirst dich *etc.* wärmen   *I shall warm myself etc.*

CONDITIONAL TENSE:

ich würde mich *etc.* wärmen   *I should warm myself etc.*

PERFECT INDICATIVE TENSE:

ich habe mich, du hast dich *etc.* gewärmt   *I have warmed myself etc.*

PLUPERFECT INDICATIVE TENSE:

ich hatte mich *etc.* gewärmt   *I had warmed myself etc.*

FUTURE PERFECT INDICATIVE TENSE:

ich werde mich, du wirst dich *etc.* gewärmt haben   *I shall have warmed myself etc.*

CONDITIONAL PERFECT TENSE:

ich würde mich *etc.* gewärmt haben   *I should have warmed myself etc.*

IMPERATIVE MOOD:

wärme dich!   *warm yourself! (fam. sing.)*
wärmt euch!   *warm yourselves! (fam. pl.)*
wärmen Sie sich!   *warm yourself* or *yourselves! (polite sing./pl.)*

SUBJUNCTIVE MOOD:

The tenses of the subjunctive mood follow the by now familiar pattern (see *fragen* above) with the addition of *mich, dich* etc.

Separable verb: einrichten

Separable verbs are verbs with accented prefixes which are generally separated from the rest of the verb in a sentence. Some examples of these prefixes are *auf-, aus-, ein-, weg-,* but there are many more. The separable prefix always goes to the end of the clause or sentence; it follows that it is normally separated from the rest of the verb in all forms except the infinitive, present participle and past participle, which also go to the end of the clause or sentence.

Many separable verbs correspond to English verbs followed by a preposition (these English verbs are known as prepositional verbs):

aufsuchen   to seek out
aufwachen   to wake up
ausgehen   to go out
eindringen   to break in

This is not always the case, however. For example:

beilegen   to enclose
sich einbilden   to imagine
einrichten   to organize

We shall take the verb *einrichten* as our model, since it is a regular verb.

INFINITIVE:

einrichten   *to organize*

PRESENT PARTICIPLE:

einrichtend   *organizing*

PAST PARTICIPLE:

eingerichtet   *organized*

Note that *ge* is inserted between the prefix and the rest of the verb. This is in contrast to verbs with inseparable prefixes, which do not add *ge* in the past participle (see 'Participles' above).

PRESENT INDICATIVE TENSE:

ich richte ein   *I organize*
du richtest ein   *you organize etc.*

PAST INDICATIVE TENSE:

ich richtete ein *etc.*   *I organized etc.*

FUTURE INDICATIVE TENSE:

ich werde, du wirst *etc.* einrichten   *I shall organize etc.*

CONDITIONAL TENSE:

ich würde *etc.* einrichten   *I should organize etc.*

PERFECT INDICATIVE TENSE:

ich habe, du hast *etc.* eingerichtet   *I have organized etc.*

PLUPERFECT INDICATIVE TENSE:

ich hatte *etc.* eingerichtet   *I had organized etc.*

FUTURE PERFECT INDICATIVE TENSE:

ich werde, du wirst *etc.* eingerichtet haben   *I shall have organized
etc.*

CONDITIONAL PERFECT TENSE:

ich würde *etc.* eingerichtet haben   *I should have organized etc.*

IMPERATIVE MOOD:

richt(e) ein!   *organize! (fam. sing.)*
richtet ein!   *organize! (fam. pl.)*
richten Sie ein!   *organize! (polite sing./pl.)*

SUBJUNCTIVE MOOD:

The subjunctive tenses follow the by now familiar pattern (see *fragen*
above).

Passive conjugation

The formation of the passive voice has been explained in the section 'Passive voice' above. Here is the complete conjugation of *fragen* in the passive.

PRESENT INDICATIVE TENSE:

ich werde gefragt   *I am asked*
du wirst gefragt *etc.*

PRESENT SUBJUNCTIVE TENSE:

ich werde gefragt
du werdest gefragt *etc.*

PAST INDICATIVE TENSE:

ich wurde gefragt   *I was asked*
du wurdest gefragt *etc.*

PAST SUBJUNCTIVE TENSE:

ich würde gefragt
du würdest gefragt *etc.*

FUTURE INDICATIVE TENSE:

ich werde gefragt werden
   I shall be asked
du wirst gefragt werden *etc.*

FUTURE SUBJUNCTIVE TENSE:

ich werde gefragt werden

du werdest gefragt werden *etc.*

CONDITIONAL TENSE:

ich würde gefragt werden   *I should be asked*
du würdest gefragt werden *etc.*

PERFECT INDICATIVE TENSE:

ich bin gefragt worden
   I have been asked
du bist gefragt worden *etc.*

PERFECT SUBJUNCTIVE TENSE:

ich sei gefragt worden

du seiest gefragt worden *etc.*

PLUPERFECT INDICATIVE TENSE:

ich war gefragt worden
   I had been asked
du warst gefragt worden *etc.*

PLUPERFECT SUBJUNCTIVE TENSE:

ich wäre gefragt worden

du wärest gefragt worden *etc.*

FUTURE PERFECT INDICATIVE
   TENSE:

ich werde gefragt worden sein
   I shall have been asked
du wirst gefragt worden sein *etc.*

FUTURE PERFECT SUBJUNCTIVE
   TENSE:

ich werde gefragt worden sein

du werdest gefragt worden sein *etc.*

CONDITIONAL PERFECT TENSE:

ich würde gefragt worden sein   *I should have been asked*
du würdest gefragt worden sein *etc.*

IMPERATIVE MOOD:

sei gefragt!   *be asked! (fam. sing.)*
seid gefragt!   *be asked! (fam pl.)*
seien Sie gefragt!   *be asked! (polite sing./pl.)*

The passive imperative is rare. Note the use of *sein* (see 'Passive voice' above).

Alternative forms

Regular and irregular conjugation

Several German verbs exist in both regular and irregular forms, with one or the other being the more common. These alternatives are indicated in the list of irregular verbs which follows.

Quite often the regular and irregular forms are differentiated in meaning. Sometimes the regular form has a figurative as well as the basic meaning. Often the regular form is used in preference when the verb is used transitively: that is, when it has a direct object. Here are some of the most common of these dual form verbs:

Infinitive	Regular forms	Irregular forms
bewegen	to move (object), stir (emotions)	to induce, move (s.o. to do sth.)
gären	to be restless	to ferment
glimmen	(of hope) to flicker	(of fire) to glimmer
hauen	to hew, beat	to aim a blow *(intransitive)*
melken	to fleece, milk	to milk
pflegen	to care for, be in the habit of	to occupy oneself with, practise
schaffen	to produce, be busy	to create
scheren	to concern, shear	to shear
senden	to broadcast, send	to send
sieden	to raise or rise to boiling point	to cook by boiling
weben	to be active, weave	to weave
wenden	*(reflexive)* to turn round	to turn (cuff etc.), turn over (page)

Regular and irregular past participle

Some verbs which are otherwise always or almost always regular have a second, irregular past participle. Generally this is used in special or figurative senses and is often used as an adjective. Here are some examples:

Infinitive	Regular past participle	Irregular past participle
bedingen	*bedingt* required, conditioned	*ein bedungener Lohn* a stipulated reward
beklemmen	*beklemmt* constricted, oppressed	*ein beklommenes Herz* a heavy heart
dingen	*gedingt* hired, engaged	*ein gedungener Mörder* a hired assassin
falten	*gefaltet* folded	*mit gefalteten Händen* with clasped hands
salzen	*gesalzt* salted	*gesalzene Preise* excessive prices
		gesalzene Witze spicy jokes
spalten	*gespaltet* split	*gespaltene Hufe* cleft hooves
verhehlen	*verhehlt* hidden	*ein verhohlener Blick* a surreptitious glance
verwirren	*verwirrt* confused	*eine verworrene Lage* a complicated situation
verwünschen	*verwünscht* cursed	*ein verwünschenes Schloß* a charmed castle

Irregular verbs

Notes on tense formation

In the list of German irregular verbs which follows, sufficient information is given to enable you to form every person of every tense correctly, if the following points are borne in mind:

1   The first and third persons are always identical except in the singular of the present tense.

2   The plural of the present tense (1st and 3rd persons) is always identical to the infinitive – with the sole exception of *sein*.

3   The polite imperative is also the same as the infinitive – again with the sole exception of *sein*.

4   The plural of the past tense is formed by adding *en* to the singular, or just *n* if the singular already ends in *e*.

Notes on the list of irregular verbs

In this list we give the forms of almost every irregular verb in the current language. The most common, and therefore the most important for you to learn first, are indicated with an asterisk.

We do not give every compound verb (that is, verbs formed by adding a separable or inseparable prefix to another verb) because they are almost invariably conjugated in the same way as the simple verb from which they are formed. Thus *ertrinken* (to drown) has the same forms as *trinken* (to drink). (The exceptions to this are few and unimportant verbs.) However, the most important of the compound verbs are included.

We have indicated those verbs which form their perfect and conditional tenses with *sein* by marking them **S**. A few verbs can take either *haben* or *sein*, and these are marked **H S**. Note that a verb always takes *haben* when it is used transitively (that is, when it has a direct object – see the section on 'Compound tenses' above).

A characteristic of many irregular German verbs is that they have a vowel change or add an umlaut in the 2nd and 3rd persons singular of the present tense. These changes and any other irregularities in the present tense are printed in bold type in the list.

Where verbs have alternative forms and can be either regular or irregular (see the section on 'Alternative forms' above) both forms are given. If one form is less usual, it is given in brackets; where no brackets appear, both forms are equally common.

List of irregular verbs

INFINITIVE:	PRESENT TENSE:
backen *to bake*	ich backe, du **bäckst**/backst, er **bäckt**/backt
bedingen *to require, condition*	ich bedinge, du bedingst, er bedingt
* befehlen *to command*	ich befehle, du **befiehlst**, er **befiehlt**
befleißen (sich) *to endeavour*	ich befleiße mich, du befleißt dich, er befleißt sich
* beginnen *to begin*	ich beginne, du beginnst, er beginnt
beißen *to bite*	ich beiße, du beißt, er beißt
bergen *to hide, salvage*	ich berge, du **birgst**, er **birgt**
bersten *to burst*	ich berste, du **birst**/berstest, er **birst**/berstet
bescheiden *to inform, summon*	ich bescheide, du bescheid(e)st, er bescheidet
besinnen (sich) *to reflect*	ich besinne mich, du besinnst dich, er besinnt sich
besitzen *to own*	ich besitze, du besitz(es)t, er besitzt
betrügen *to deceive*	ich betrüge, du betrügst, er betrügt
bewegen *to induce*	ich bewege, du bewegst, er bewegt
* biegen *to bend*	ich biege, du biegst, er biegt
bieten *to offer*	ich biete, du biet(e)st, er bietet
* binden *to bind*	ich binde, du bind(e)st, er bindet
* bitten *to beg, request*	ich bitte, du bittest, er bittet

PAST TENSE:	PAST PARTICIPLE:
buk/backte	gebacken
bedingte (bedang)	bedingt (bedungen) *(see 'Alternative Forms')*
befahl *subjunctive* beföhle (befähle)	befohlen
befliß	beflissen
begann *subjunctive* begönne (begänne)	begonnen
biß	gebissen
barg	geborgen
barst	geborsten **S**
beschied	beschieden
besann *subjunctive* besönne (besänne)	besonnen
besaß	besessen
betrog	betrogen
bewog/bewegte	bewogen/bewegt *(see 'Alternative forms')*
bog	gebogen
bot	geboten
band	gebunden
bat	gebeten

INFINITIVE:	PRESENT TENSE:
* blasen *to blow*	ich blase, du **bläs(es)t**, er **bläst**
* bleiben *to remain*	ich bleibe, du bleibst, er bleibt
bleichen *to turn pale*	ich bleiche, du bleichst, er bleicht
braten *to fry, roast*	ich brate, du **brätst**, er **brät**
* brechen *to break*	ich breche, du **brichst**, er **bricht**
* brennen *to burn*	ich brenne, du brennst, er brennt
* bringen *to bring*	ich bringe, du bringst, er bringt
* denken *to think*	ich denke, du denkst, er denkt
dingen *to engage (a servant)*	ich dinge, du dingst, er dingt
dreschen *to thrash*	ich dresche, du **drisch(e)st**, er **drischt**
dringen *to urge*	ich dringe, du dringst, er dringt
* dürfen *to be allowed*	ich **darf**, du **darfst**, er **darf**
* empfangen *to receive*	ich empfange, du **empfängst**, er **empfängt**
* empfehlen *to recommend*	ich empfehle, du **empfiehlst**, er **empfiehlt**
empfinden *to feel*	ich empfinde, du empfind(e)st, er empfindet
entrinnen *to escape*	ich entrinne, du entrinnst, er entrinnt
erbleichen *to grow pale, die away*	ich erbleiche, du erbleichst, er erbleicht
erküren *to elect*	ich erküre, du erkürst, er erkürt
erlöschen *to go out (of a light)*	ich erlösche, du **erlischst**, er **erlischt** *used transitively* er erlöscht
erschallen *to resound*	ich erschalle, du erschallst, er erschallt

PAST TENSE:	PAST PARTICIPLE:
blies	geblasen
blieb	geblieben **S**
blich/bleichte	geblichen/gebleicht **S**
briet	gebraten
brach	gebrochen **H S**
brannte	gebrannt
brachte	gebracht
dachte	gedacht
dingte (dang)	gedungen (gedingt) *(see 'Alternative forms')*
drosch/drasch	gedroschen
drang	gedrungen
durfte	gedurft
empfing	empfangen
empfahl *subjunctive* empföhle (empfähle)	empfohlen
empfand	empfunden
entrann	entronnen **S**
erblich/erbleichte	erblichen **S**/erbleicht
erkor	erkoren
erlosch	erloschen **H S**
erschallte (erscholl)	erschallt/erschollen **S**

INFINITIVE:	PRESENT TENSE:
erschrecken *to be startled*	ich erschrecke, du **erschrickst**, er **erschrickt** *reflexive* er erschreckt sich
ertrinken *to be drowned*	ich ertrinke, du ertrinkst, er ertrinkt
erwägen *to consider*	ich erwäge, du erwägst, er erwägt
* essen *to eat*	ich esse, du **ißt**, er **ißt**
* fahren *to travel (in a vehicle)*	ich fahre, du **fährst**, er **fährt**
* fallen *to fall*	ich falle, du **fällst**, er **fällt**
* fangen *to catch*	ich fange, du **fängst**, er **fängt**
fechten *to fence, fight*	ich fechte, du **fichtst**, er **ficht**
* finden *to find*	ich finde, du find(e)st, er findet
flechten *to plait*	ich flechte, du **flichtst**, er **flicht**
* fliegen *to fly*	ich fliege, du fliegst, er fliegt
fliehen *to flee*	ich fliehe, du fliehst, er flieht
* fließen *to flow*	ich fließe, du fließ(es)t, er fließt
fressen *to eat (speaking of animals)*	ich fresse, du **frißt**, er **frißt**
frieren *to freeze*	ich friere, du frierst, er friert
gären *to ferment*	ich gäre, du gärst, er gärt
gebären *to bear, give birth to*	ich gebäre, du **gebierst**/gebärst, er **gebiert**/gebärt
* geben *to give*	ich gebe, du **gibst**, er **gibt**
gebieten *to command*	ich gebiete, du gebiet(e)st, er gebietet
gedeihen *to thrive*	ich gedeihe, du gedeihst, er gedeiht

PAST TENSE:	PAST PARTICIPLE:
erschrak/erschreckte sich	erschrocken **S**/erschreckt
ertrank	ertrunken **S**
erwog	erwogen
aß	gegessen
fuhr	gefahren **H S**
fiel	gefallen **S**
fing	gefangen
focht	gefochten
fand	gefunden
flocht	geflochten
flog	geflogen **S**
floh	geflohen **S**
floß	geflossen **S**
fraß	gefressen
fror	gefroren **H S**
gor/gärte	gegoren/gegärt *(see 'Alternative forms')*
gebar	geboren
gab	gegeben
gebot	geboten
gedieh	gediehen **S**

INFINITIVE:	PRESENT TENSE:
gefallen *to please*	ich gefalle, du **gefällst**, er **gefällt**
* gehen *to go*	ich gehe, du gehst, er geht
gelingen *to succeed*	es gelingt (mir *etc.*)
gelten *to be valid*	ich gelte, du **giltst**, er **gilt**
genesen *to convalesce*	ich genese, du genes(es)t, er genest
genießen *to enjoy, eat*	ich genieße, du genieß(es)t, er genießt
geraten *to turn out*	ich gerate, du **gerätst**, er **gerät**
geschehen *to happen*	es **geschieht**
gewinnen *to win*	ich gewinne, du gewinnst, er gewinnt
gießen *to pour*	ich gieße, du gieß(es)t, er gießt
gleichen *to resemble, equalize*	ich gleiche, du gleichst, er gleicht
gleiten *to glide, slide*	ich gleite, du gleitst, er gleitet
glimmen *to glimmer*	ich glimme, du glimmst, er glimmt
graben *to dig*	ich grabe, du **gräbst**, er **gräbt**
greifen *to grasp*	ich greife, du greifst, er greift
* haben *to have*	ich habe, du **hast**, er **hat**
* halten *to hold*	ich halte, du **hältst**, er **hält**
hängen (hangen) *to hang*	ich hänge (hange), du hängst, er hängt
hauen *to aim a blow, beat*	ich haue, du haust, er haut

PAST TENSE:	PAST PARTICIPLE:
gefiel	gefallen
ging	gegangen **S**
gelang	gelungen **S**
galt	gegolten
subjunctive gölte (gälte)	
genas	genesen **S**
genoß	genossen
geriet	geraten **S**
geschah	geschehen **S**
gewann	gewonnen
subjunctive gewönne	
(gewänne)	
goß	gegossen
glich	geglichen
glitt	geglitten **S**
glomm/glimmte	geglommen/geglimmt
	(see 'Alternative forms')
grub	gegraben
griff	gegriffen
hatte	gehabt
hielt	gehalten
hing	gehangen
hieb/haute	gehauen/gehaut
	(see 'Alternative forms')

INFINITIVE:		PRESENT TENSE:
heben	*to lift*	ich hebe, du hebst, er hebt
* heißen	*to be called, bid*	ich heiße, du heiß(es)t, er heißt
* helfen	*to help*	ich helfe, du **hilfst**, er **hilft**
* kennen	*to know*	ich kenne, du kennst, er kennt
klieben	*to split*	ich kliebe, du kliebst, er kliebt
klimmen	*to climb*	ich klimme, du klimmst, er klimmt
klingen	*to sound*	ich klinge, du klingst, er klingt
kneifen	*to pinch*	ich kneife, du kneifst, er kneift
* kommen	*to come*	ich komme, du kommst, er kommt
* können	*to be able to*	ich **kann**, du **kannst**, er **kann**
kriechen	*to creep*	ich krieche, du kriechst, er kriecht
küren	*to choose*	ich küre, du kürst, er kürt
laden	*to load*	ich lade, du **lädst**/ladest, er **lädt**/ladet
* lassen	*to let, leave*	ich lasse, du **läßt**, er **läßt**
* laufen	*to run*	ich laufe, du **läufst**, er **läuft**
leiden	*to suffer*	ich leide, du leidest, er leidet
* leihen	*to lend*	ich leihe, du leihst, er leiht
* lesen	*to read*	ich lese, du **liest**, er **liest**
* liegen	*to lie*	ich liege, du liegst, er liegt
* lügen	*to tell lies*	ich lüge, du lügst, er lügt
mahlen	*to grind*	ich mahle, du mahlst, er mahlt
meiden	*to avoid*	ich meide, du meidest, er meidet

PAST TENSE:	PAST PARTICIPLE:
hob	gehoben
hieß	geheißen
half	geholfen
subjunctive hülfe (hälfe)	
kannte	gekannt
klob/kliebte	gekloben/gekliebt
klomm/klimmte	geklommen/geklimmt **S**
klang	geklungen
kniff	gekniffen
kam	gekommen **S**
konnte	gekonnt
kroch	gekrochen **S**
kor/kürte	gekoren
lud/ladete	geladen
ließ	gelassen
lief	gelaufen **S**
litt	gelitten
lieh	geliehen
las	gelesen
lag	gelegen **H S**
log	gelogen
mahlte	gemahlen
mied	gemieden

INFINITIVE:	PRESENT TENSE:
melken *to milk*	ich melke, du melkst (**milkst**), er melkt (**milkt**)
messen *to measure*	ich messe, du **mißt**, er **mißt**
mißlingen *to fail*	ich mißlinge, du mißlingst, er mißlingt
* mögen *to like (to)*	ich **mag**, du **magst**, er **mag**
* müssen *to have to*	ich **muß**, du **mußt**, er **muß**
* nehmen *to take*	ich nehme, du **nimmst**, er **nimmt**
nennen *to name*	ich nenne, du nennst, er nennt
pfeifen *to whistle*	ich pfeife, du pfeifst, er pfeift
pflegen *to occupy* *oneself with, care for*	ich pflege, du pflegst, er pflegt
preisen *to praise*	ich preise, du preis(es)t, er preist
quellen *to bubble up*	ich quelle, du **quillst**, er **quillt**
raten *to advise*	ich rate, du **rätst**, er **rät**
reiben *to rub*	ich reibe, du reibst, er reibt
reißen *to tear*	ich reiße, du reiß(es)t, er reißt
reiten *to ride (on an* *animal)*	ich reite, du reit(e)st, er reitet
* rennen *to run, race*	ich renne, du rennst, er rennt
riechen *to smell*	ich rieche, du riechst, er riecht
ringen *to wrestle*	ich ringe, du ringst, er ringt
rinnen *to leak, flow*	ich rinne, du rinnst, er rinnt
* rufen *to call, shout*	ich rufe, du rufst, er ruft
salzen *to salt*	ich salze, du salz(es)t, er salzt

PAST TENSE:	PAST PARTICIPLE:
melkte (molk)	gemolken (gemelkt) *(see 'Alternative forms')*
maß	gemessen
mißlang	mißlungen **S**
mochte	gemocht
mußte	gemußt
nahm	genommen
nannte	genannt
pfiff	gepfiffen
pflog/pflegte	gepflogen/gepflegt *(see 'Alternative forms')*
pries	gepriesen
quoll	gequollen **S**
riet	geraten
rieb	gerieben
riß	gerissen
ritt	geritten **H S**
rannte	gerannt **S**
roch	gerochen
rang	gerungen
rann	geronnen **H S**
rief	gerufen
salzte	gesalzen/gesalzt *(see 'Alternative forms')*

INFINITIVE:	PRESENT TENSE:
saufen *to swill*	ich saufe, du **säufst**, er **säuft**
saugen *to suck*	ich sauge, du saugst, er saugt
schaffen *to create, be busy*	ich schaffe, du schaffst, er schafft
scheiden *to part*	ich scheide, du scheid(e)st, er scheidet
* scheinen *to seem, shine*	ich scheine, du scheinst, er scheint
scheißen *to shit*	ich scheiße, du scheiß(es)t, er scheißt
schelten *to scold*	ich schelte, du **schiltst**, er **schilt**
scheren *to shear, concern*	ich schere, du scherst (**schierst**), er schert (**schiert**)
schieben *to push*	ich schiebe, du schiebst, er schiebt
* schießen *to shoot, shoot forth*	ich schieße, du schieß(es)t, er schießt
schinden *to flay*	ich schinde, du schind(e)st, er schindet
* schlafen *to sleep*	ich schlafe, du **schläfst**, er **schläft**
* schlagen *to beat, strike*	ich schlage, du **schlägst**, er **schlägt**
schleichen *to slink, creep*	ich schleiche, du schleichst, er schleicht
schleifen *to sharpen*	ich schleife, du schleifst, er schleift
schleißen *to slit*	ich schleiße, du schleiß(es)t, er schleißt
* schließen *to shut*	ich schließe, du schließ(es)t, er schließt
schlingen *to wind, swallow*	ich schlinge, du schlingst, er schlingt
schmeißen *to fling, chuck*	ich schmeiße, du schmeiß(es)t, er schmeißt

PAST TENSE:	PAST PARTICIPLE:
soff	gesoffen
sog (saugte)	gesogen (gesaugt)
schuf/schaffte	geschaffen/geschafft *(see 'Alternative forms')*
schied	geschieden **H S**
schien	geschienen
schiß	geschissen
schalt *subjunctive* schölte (schälte)	gescholten
schor/scherte	geschoren/geschert *(see 'Alternative forms')*
schob	geschoben
schoß	geschossen **H S**
schund (schindete)	geschunden
schlief	geschlafen
schlug	geschlagen
schlich	geschlichen **S**
schliff/schleifte	geschliffen/geschleift
schliß/schleißte	geschlissen/geschleißt
schloß	geschlossen
schlang	geschlungen
schmiß	geschmissen

INFINITIVE:	PRESENT TENSE:
schmelzen *to melt* (intransitive)	ich schmelze, du **schmilz(es)t**, er **schmilzt**
schnauben *to snort*	ich schnaube, du schnaubst, er schnaubt
* schneiden *to cut*	ich schneide, du schneid(e)st, er schneidet
schrauben *to screw*	ich schraube, du schraubst, er schraubt
schrecken *to be* frightened	ich schrecke, du **schrickst**, er **schrickt**
* schreiben *to write*	ich schreibe, du schreibst, er schreibt
schreien *to scream, shout*	ich schreie, du schrei(e)st, er schreit
schreiten *to stride, step*	ich schreite, du schreit(e)st, er schreitet
schwären *to fester*	ich schwäre, du schwärst, er schwärt
schweigen *to be silent*	ich schweige, du schweigst, er schweigt
schwellen *to swell*	ich schwelle, du **schwillst**, er **schwillt**
* schwimmen *to swim*	ich schwimme, du schwimmst, er schwimmt
schwinden *to shrink, dwindle*	ich schwinde, du schwind(e)st, er schwindet
schwingen *to swing*	ich schwinge, du schwingst, er schwingt
schwören *to swear* (on oath)	ich schwöre, du schwörst, er schwört
* sehen *to see*	ich sehe, du **siehst**, er **sieht**
* sein *to be*	ich bin, du **bist**, er **ist**, wir **sind**, ihr **seid**, sie **sind**
* senden *to send*	ich sende, du send(e)st, er sendet

PAST TENSE:	PAST PARTICIPLE:
schmolz	geschmolzen **S**
schnaubte (schnob)	geschnaubt (geschnoben)
schnitt	geschnitten
schraubte	geschraubt
schrak	erschrocken **S**
schrieb	geschrieben
schrie	geschrie(e)n
schritt	geschritten **S**
schwärte (schwor)	geschwärt (geschworen)
schwieg	geschwiegen
schwoll	geschwollen **S**
schwamm *subjunctive* schwömme/ schwämme	geschwommen **H S**
schwand	geschwunden **S**
schwang	geschwungen
schwor/schwur *subjunctive* schwüre	geschworen
sah	gesehen
war	gewesen **S**
sandte/sendete	gesandt/gesendet *(see 'Alternative forms')*

INFINITIVE:		PRESENT TENSE:
sieden	*to boil*	ich siede, du sied(e)st, er siedet
* singen	*to sing*	ich singe, du singst, er singt
sinken	*to sink*	ich sinke, du sinkst, er sinkt
sinnen	*to ponder*	ich sinne, du sinnst, er sinnt
* sitzen	*to sit, be sitting*	ich sitze, du sitz(es)t, er sitzt
* sollen	*ought, should*	ich **soll,** du **sollst,** er **soll**
speien	*to spit*	ich speie, du spei(e)st, er speit
spinnen	*to spin*	ich spinne, du spinnest, er spinnt
spleißen	*to split*	ich spleiße, du spleiß(es)t, er spleißt
* sprechen	*to speak*	ich spreche, du **sprichst,** er **spricht**
sprießen	*to sprout*	ich sprieße, du sprieß(es)t, er sprießt
springen	*to spring, jump*	ich springe, du springst, er springt
stechen	*to sting, stab*	ich steche, du **stichst,** er **sticht**
stecken	*to stick, put*	ich stecke, du steckst, er steckt
* stehen	*to stand*	ich stehe, du stehst, er steht
stehlen	*to steal*	ich stehle, du **stiehlst,** er **stiehlt**
* steigen	*to ascend, climb*	ich steige, du steigst, er steigt
sterben	*to die*	ich sterbe, du **stirbst,** er **stirbt**
stieben	*to fly (of sparks)*	ich stiebe, du stiebst, er stiebt
stinken	*to stink*	ich stinke, du stinkst, er stinkt

PAST TENSE:	PAST PARTICIPLE:
sott/siedete	gesotten/gesiedet *(see 'Alternative forms')*
sang	gesungen
sank	gesunken **S**
sann *subjunctive* sönne (sänne)	gesonnen
saß	gesessen **H S**
sollte	gesollt
spie	gespie(e)n
spann *subjunctive* spönne (spänne)	gesponnen
spliß (spleißte)	gesplissen **S** (gespleißt)
sprach	gesprochen
sproß	gesprossen **S**
sprang	gesprungen **S**
stach	gestochen
steckte (stak)	gesteckt
stand	gestanden **H S**
stahl	gestohlen
stieg	gestiegen **S**
starb *subjunctive* stürbe	gestorben **S**
stob (stiebte)	gestoben **S**
stank	gestunken

INFINITIVE:	PRESENT TENSE:
stoßen *to push, shove*	ich stoße, du **stöß(es)t,** er **stößt**
streichen *to wander, cross out*	ich streiche, du streichst, er streicht
streiten *to quarrel*	ich streite, du streitst, er streitet
* tragen *to carry, wear*	ich trage, du **trägst,** er **trägt**
* treffen *to hit, meet*	ich treffe, du **triffst,** er **trifft**
treiben *to drive, drift*	ich treibe, du treibst, er treibt
* treten *to tread*	ich trete, du **trittst,** er **tritt**
triefen *to drip*	ich triefe, du triefst, er trieft
* trinken *to drink*	ich trinke, du trinkst, er trinkt
trügen *to mislead*	ich trüge, du trügst, er trügt
* tun *to do*	ich tue, du tust, er tut
verbergen *to hide*	ich verberge, du **verbirgst,** er **verbirgt**
verbieten *to forbid*	ich verbiete, du verbiet(e)st, er verbietet
verderben *to spoil*	ich verderbe, du **verdirbst,** er **verdirbt**
verdrießen *to vex, annoy*	ich verdrieße, du verdrieß(es)t, er verdrießt
' vergessen *to forget*	ich vergesse, du **vergißt,** er **vergißt**
* verlieren *to lose*	ich verliere, du verlierst, er verliert
* verschließen *to lock*	ich verschließe, du verschließ(es)t, er verschließt
verzeihen *to forgive*	ich verzeihe, du verzeihst, er verzeiht
wachsen *to grow*	ich wachse, du **wächst,** er **wächst**
wägen *to weigh, ponder*	ich wäge, du wägst, er wägt

PAST TENSE:	PAST PARTICIPLE:
stieß	gestoßen
strich	gestrichen
stritt	gestritten
trug	getragen
traf	getroffen
trieb	getrieben
trat	getreten **S**
triefte (troff)	getrieft (getroffen)
trank	getrunken
trog	getrogen
tat	getan
verbarg	verborgen
verbot	verboten
verdarb *subjunctive* verdürbe	verdorben
verdroß	verdrossen
vergaß	vergessen
verlor	verloren
verschloß	verschlossen
verzieh (verzeihte)	verziehen
wuchs	gewachsen **S**
wog	gewogen

INFINITIVE:		PRESENT TENSE:
* waschen	to wash	ich wasche, du **wäsch(es)t**, er **wäscht**
weben	to weave, be active	ich webe, du webst, er webt
weichen	to yield, give way	ich weiche, du weichst, er weicht
* weisen	to show	ich weise, du weis(es)t, er weist
* wenden	to turn	ich wende, du wendest, er wendet
werben	to woo, enlist	ich werbe, du **wirbst**, er **wirbt**
* werden	to become	ich werde, du **wirst,** er **wird**
* werfen	to throw	ich werfe, du **wirfst,** er **wirft**
wiegen	to weigh	ich wiege, du wiegst, er wiegt
winden	to wind	ich winde, du windest, er windet
* wissen	to know (how to)	ich **weiß,** du **weißt,** er **weiß**
* wollen	to want (to)	ich **will,** du **willst,** er **will**
wringen	to wring	ich wringe, du wringst, er wringt
zeihen	to accuse	ich zeihe, du zeihst, er zeiht
* ziehen	to draw, pull	ich ziehe, du ziehst, er zieht
* zwingen	to force	ich zwinge, du zwingst, er zwingt

86

PAST TENSE:	PAST PARTICIPLE:
wusch	gewaschen
webte (wob)	gewebt (gewoben) *(see 'Alternative forms')*
wich	gewichen **S**
wies	gewiesen
wandte/wendete	gewandt/gewendet *(see 'Alternative forms')*
warb *subjunctive* würbe	geworben
wurde (ward)	geworden **S** *in passive* worden
warf	geworfen
wog	gewogen
wand	gewunden
wußte	gewußt
wollte	gewollt
wrang	gewrungen
zieh (zeihte)	geziehen
zog	gezogen
zwang	gezwungen

Groups of irregular verbs

Most of the verbs in the preceding list can be divided into groups according to the vowels in the stem; verbs marked * below have slight additional irregularities.

e/a/a

These verbs take *a* in the past tense and in the past participle, but retain the regular endings:

brennen, kennen, nennen, rennen, senden, wenden

ei/ie/ie

bleiben, gedeihen, leihen, meiden, preisen, reiben, scheiden, scheinen, schreiben, schreien, schweigen, speien, steigen, treiben, verzeihen, weisen, zeihen

ei/i/i

beißen, erbleichen, gleichen, gleiten*, greifen*, kneifen*, leiden*, pfeifen*, reißen, reiten*, schleichen, schleifen*, schleißen, schmeißen, schneiden*, schreiten*, spleißen, streichen, streiten*, weichen

ie or e or ö or ü or ä or au/o/o

betrügen, bewegen, biegen, bieten, dreschen, erküren, (v)erlöschen, erschallen, fechten, flechten, fliegen, fliehen, fließen, frieren, gären, genießen, gießen, glimmen, heben, klimmen, kriechen, lügen, melken, pflegen, quellen, riechen, saufen, saugen, scheren, schieben, schießen, schließen, schmelzen, schnauben, schrauben, schwellen, schwören, sieden*, sprießen, stieben, triefen*, trügen, verbieten, verdrießen, verlieren, verschließen, wägen, weben, wiegen, ziehen*

i/a/u

binden, dingen, dringen, empfinden, finden, gelingen, klingen, mißlingen, ringen, schlingen, schwinden, schwingen, singen, sinken, springen, stinken, trinken, winden, wringen, zwingen

a/u/a

These verbs also have an umlaut in the 2nd and 3rd persons singular of the present tense:

backen, fahren, graben, laden, schlagen, tragen, wachsen, waschen

a/ie/a

These verbs also have an umlaut in the 2nd and 3rd persons singular of the present tense:

blasen, braten*, fallen*, gefallen*, geraten*, halten*, lassen, laufen, raten*, schlafen

a or e/i/a

With the exception of *gehen*, these verbs have an umlaut in the 2nd and 3rd persons singular of the present tense:

empfangen, fangen, gehen, hangen

e or ie or i/a/e

The following verbs have a vowel change in the 2nd and 3rd persons singular of the present tense:

essen*, fressen, geben, geschehen, lesen, messen, sehen, treten*, vergessen

The following verbs do not:

besitzen*, bitten*, genesen, liegen, sitzen*

ä or e/i/o

The following verbs have a vowel change in the 2nd and 3rd persons singular of the present tense:

befehlen, bergen, bersten, brechen, empfehlen, erschrecken, gebären, gelten*, helfen, nehmen*, schelten, sprechen, stechen, stehlen, sterben, treffen*, verbergen, verderben, werben, werfen

The following verbs do not:

beginnen, entrinnen, gewinnen, rinnen, schwimmen, sinnen, spinnen